Transcribed by CARL CULPEPPER

CONTENTS

RANCID – AND OUT COME THE WOLVES

- 77 As Wicked
- 80 Avenues & Alleyways
- 48 Daly City Train
- 64 Disorder and Disarray
- 10 The 11th Hour
- 52 Journey to the End of the East Bay
- 35 Junkie Man
- 40 Listed M.I.A.
- 29 Lock, Step & Gone
- 7 Maxwell Murder
- 60 Old Friend
- 24 Olympia Wa.
- 15 Roots Radicals
- 44 Ruby Soho
- 56 She's Automatic
- 21 Time Bomb
- 69 The Wars End
- 85 The Way I Feel
- 72 You Don't Care Nothin'

RANCID
- 90 Adina

RANCID – LET'S GO
- 111 The Ballad of Jimmy & Johnny
- 94 Nihilism
- 98 Radio
- 107 Salvation
- 103 Side Kick
- 115 St. Mary
- 120 Guitar Notation Legend

Pages 2-6 designed by Jesse Fischer and Tim Armstrong.

ISBN 978-0-7935-7242-7

7777 W. BLUEMOUND RD. P.O. BOX 13819 MILWAUKEE, WI 53213

For all works contained herein:
Unauthorized copying, arranging, adapting, recording or public performance is an infringement of copyright. Infringers are liable under the law.

Visit Hal Leonard Online at
www.halleonard.com

Angry voices, swelling crowds, and a tense incident erupt into violence—a riot begins. In cities, on college campuses, even in high schools, discontent and frustration born out of a growing sense of powerlessness have galvanized people into acts of open rebellion. Authority, the "system," the establishment—these are the targets under attack

Maxwell Murder

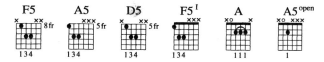

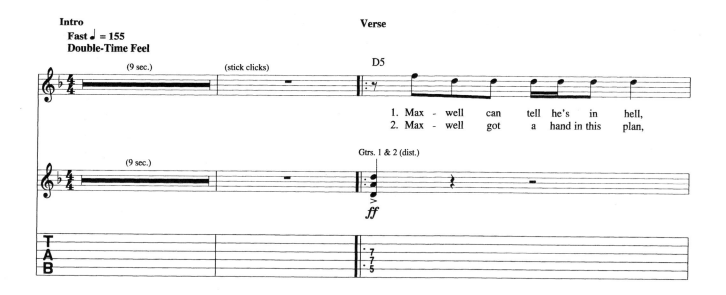

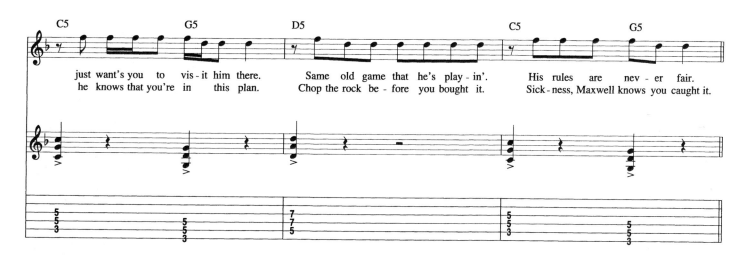

Copyright © 1995 I Want To Go Where The Action Is Music (BMI)
All Rights Administered by Wixen Music Publishing, Inc.
International Copyright Secured   All Rights Reserved

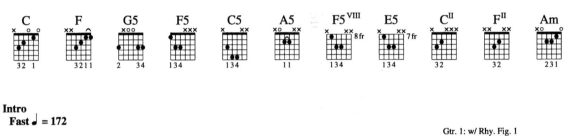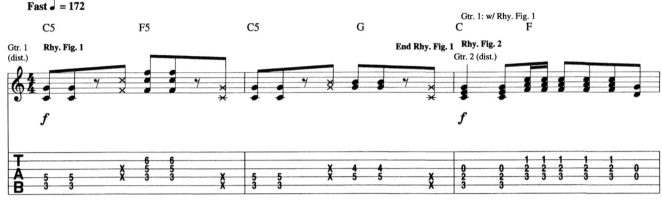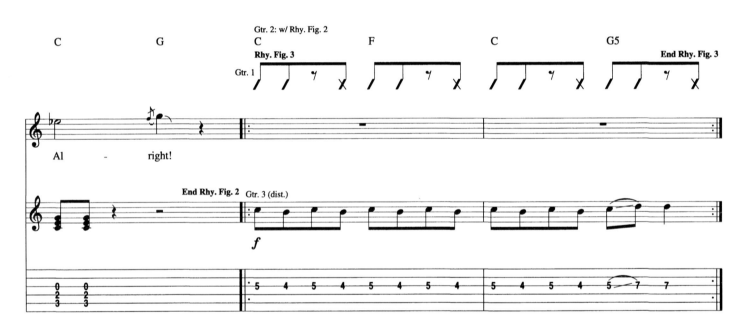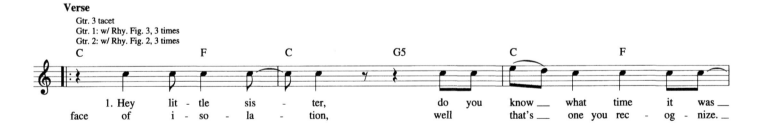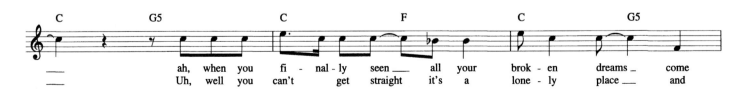

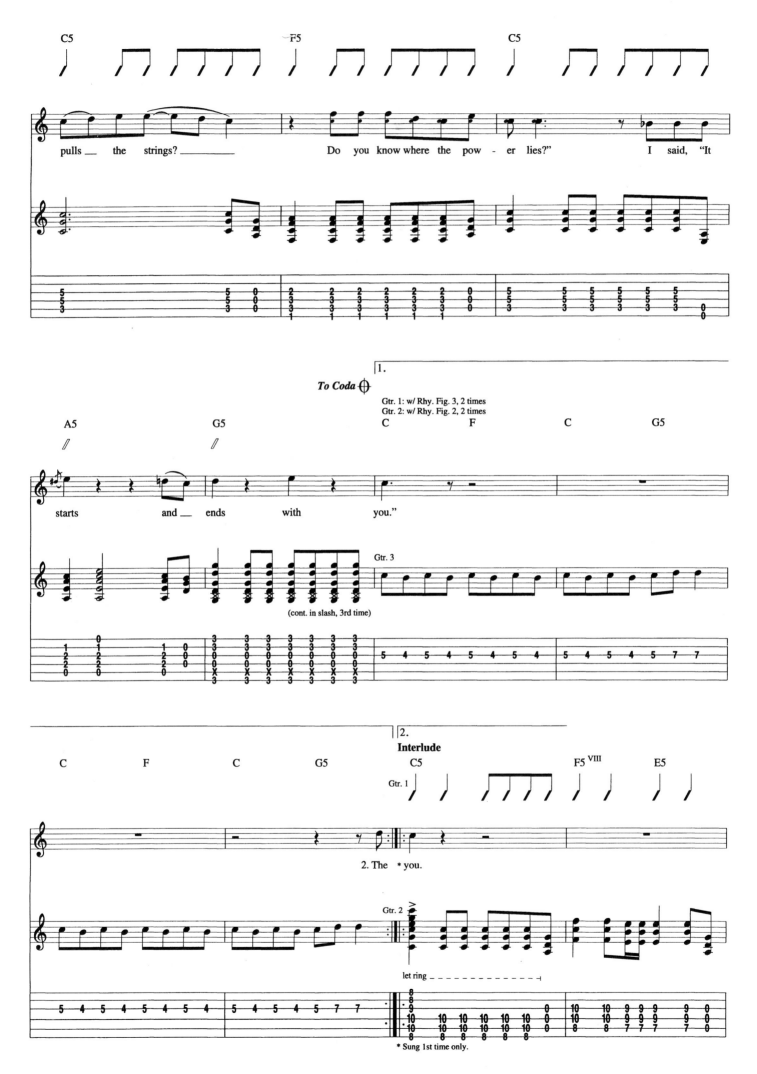

Roots Radicals

Words and Music by Tim Armstrong, Matt Freeman and Lars Frederiksen

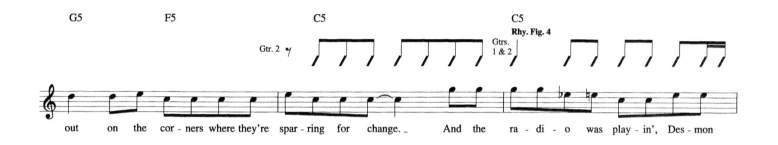
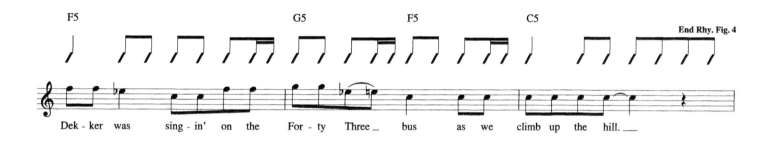
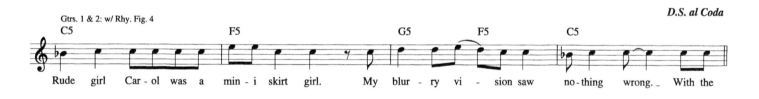

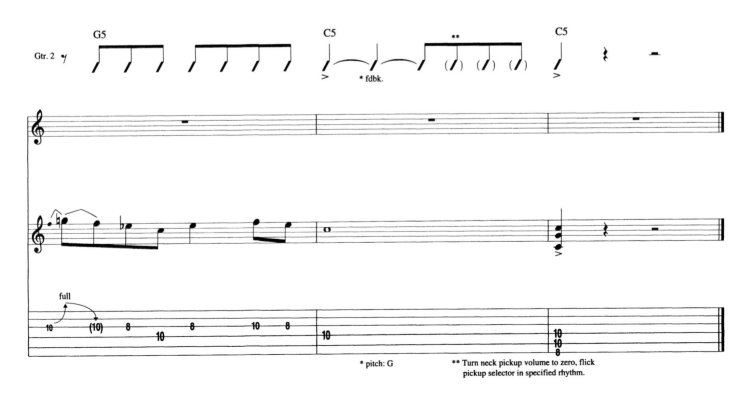

* pitch: G ** Turn neck pickup volume to zero, flick pickup selector in specified rhythm.

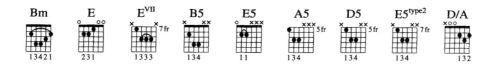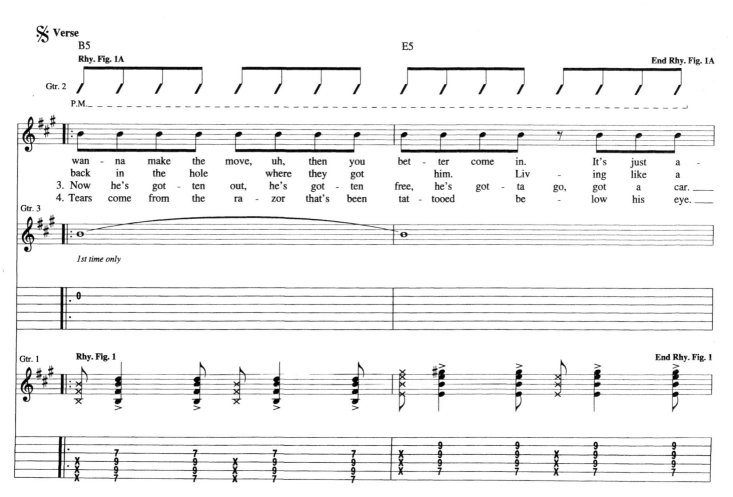

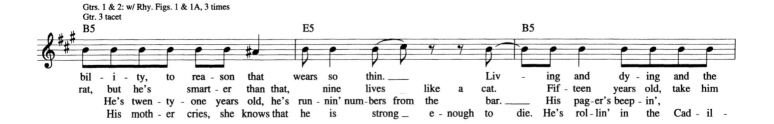
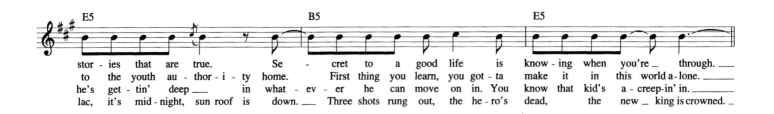
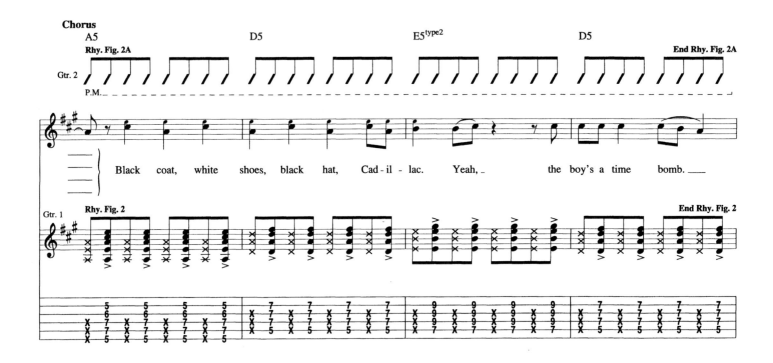

Olympia Wa.

Words and Music by Tim Armstrong, Matt Freeman and Lars Frederiksen

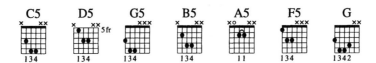

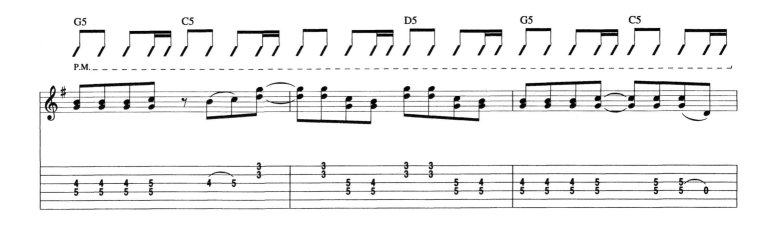

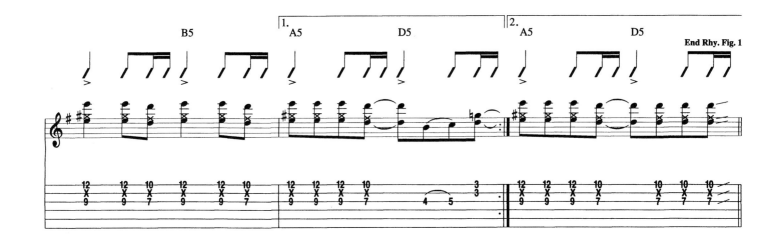

Copyright © 1995 I Want To Go Where The Action Is Music (BMI)
All Rights Administered by Wixen Music Publishing, Inc.
International Copyright Secured   All Rights Reserved

Lock, Step & Gone

Words and Music by Tim Armstrong, Matt Freeman and Lars Frederiksen

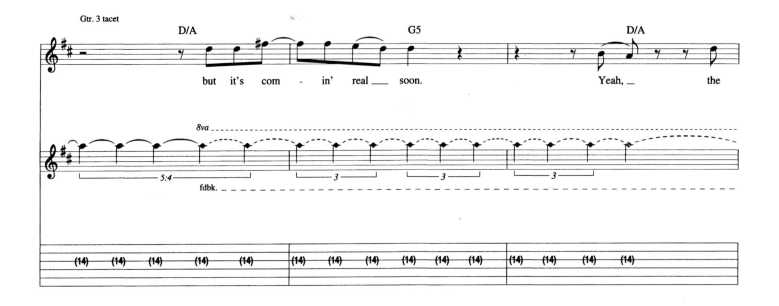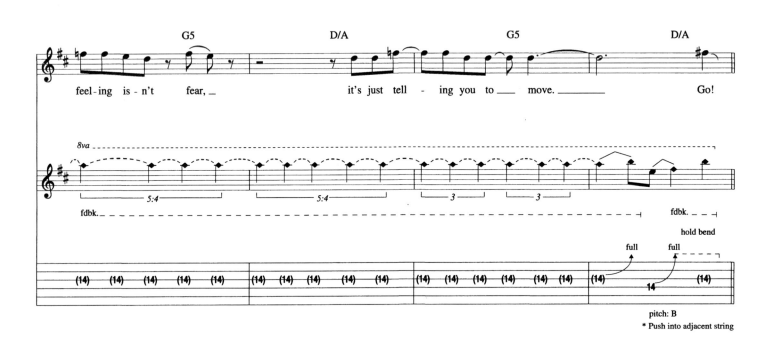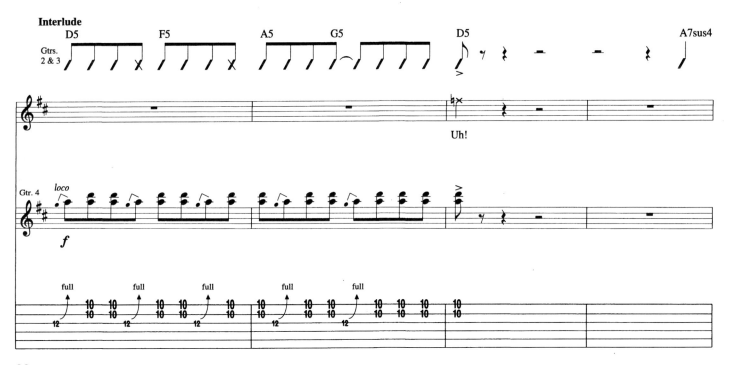

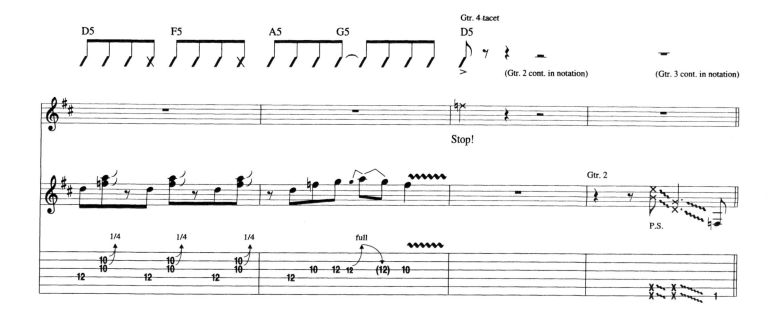

Chorus

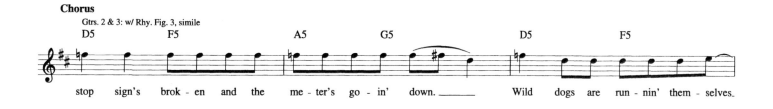

stop sign's brok-en and the me-ter's go-in' down. Wild dogs are run-nin' them-selves

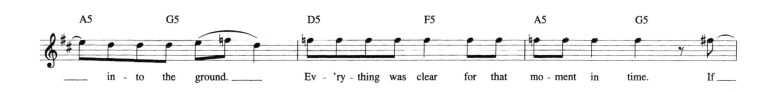

in-to the ground. Ev-'ry-thing was clear for that mo-ment in time. If

D.S. al Coda

I don't come back, well, throw me a line. 4. All the

33

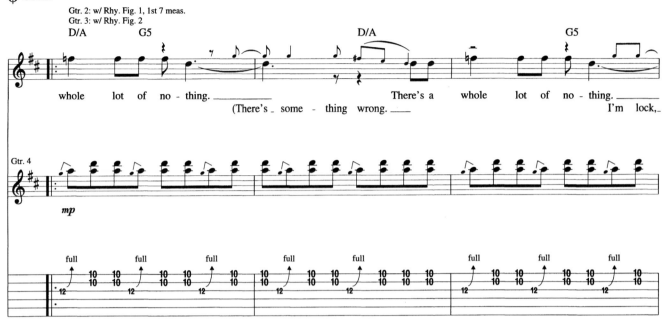

Listed M.I.A.

Words and Music by Tim Armstrong, Matt Freeman and Lars Frederiksen

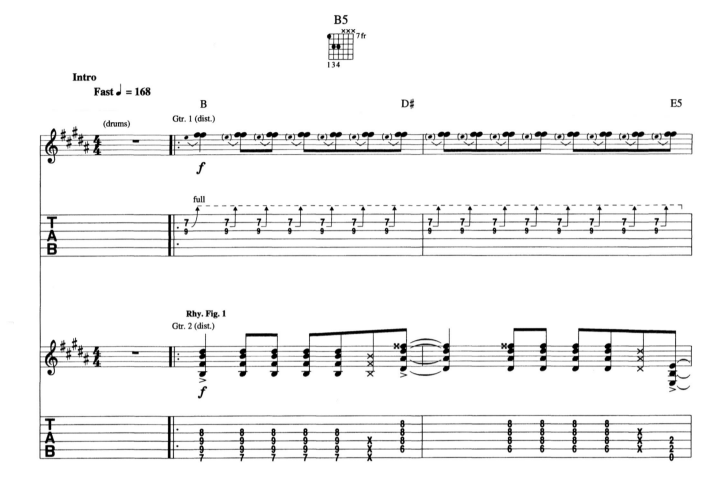

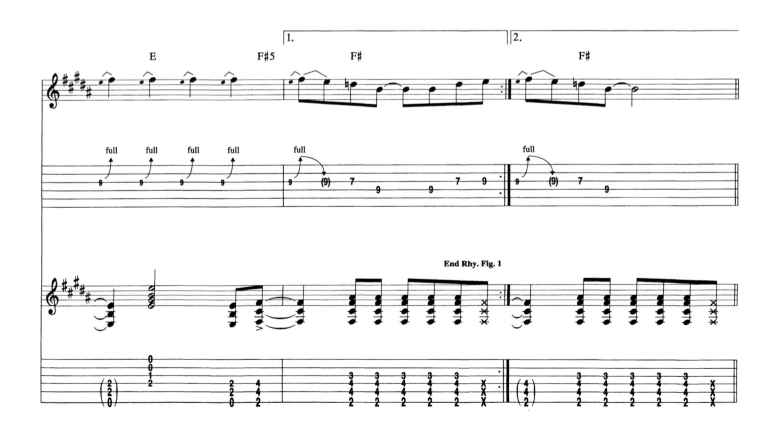

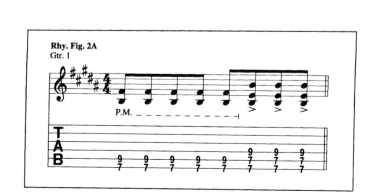

Ruby Soho

Words and Music by Tim Armstrong, Matt Freeman and Lars Frederiksen

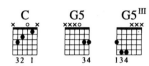

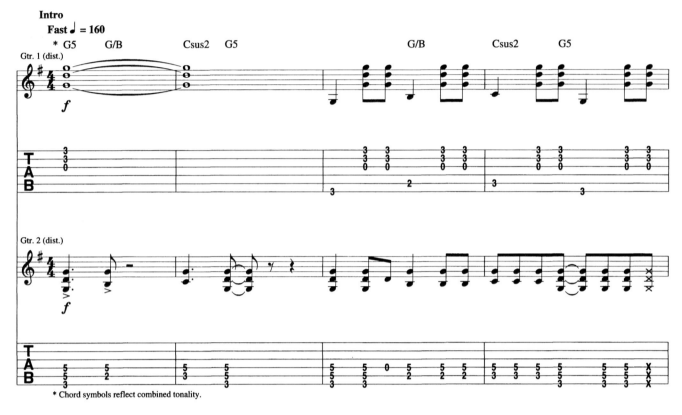

* Chord symbols reflect combined tonality.

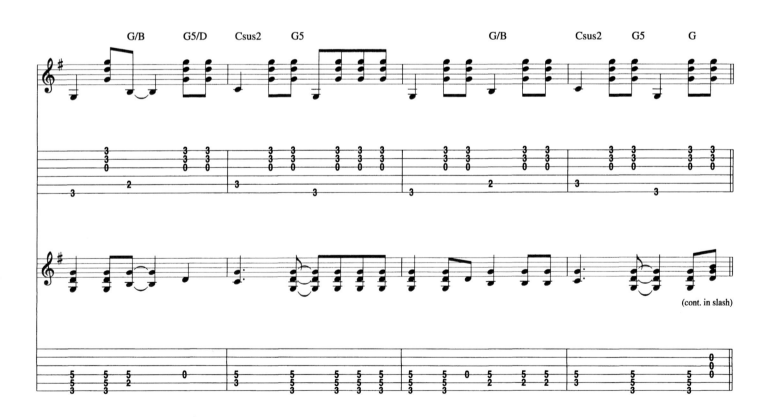

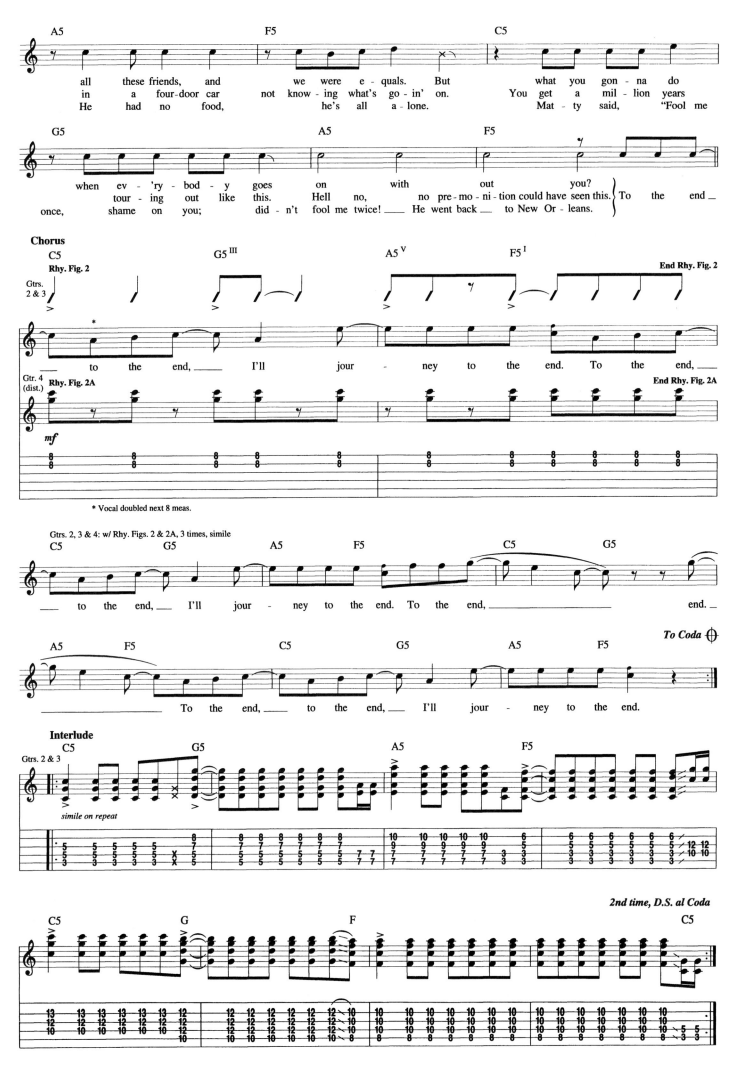

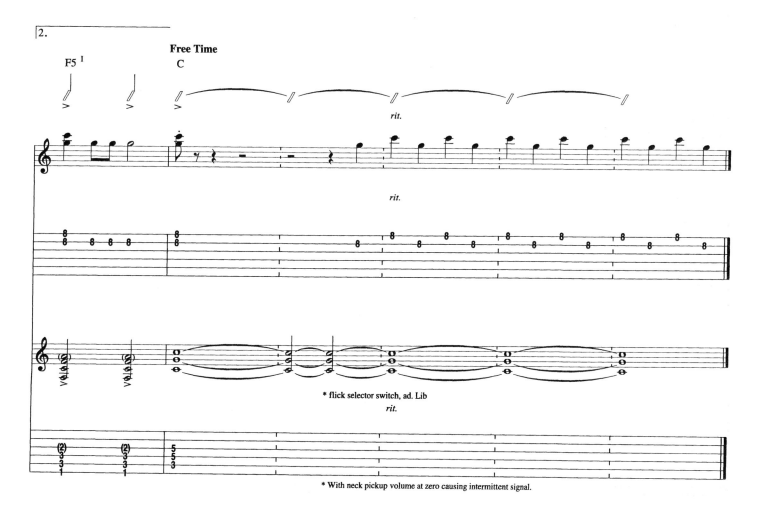

*flick selector switch, ad. Lib

*With neck pickup volume at zero causing intermittent signal.

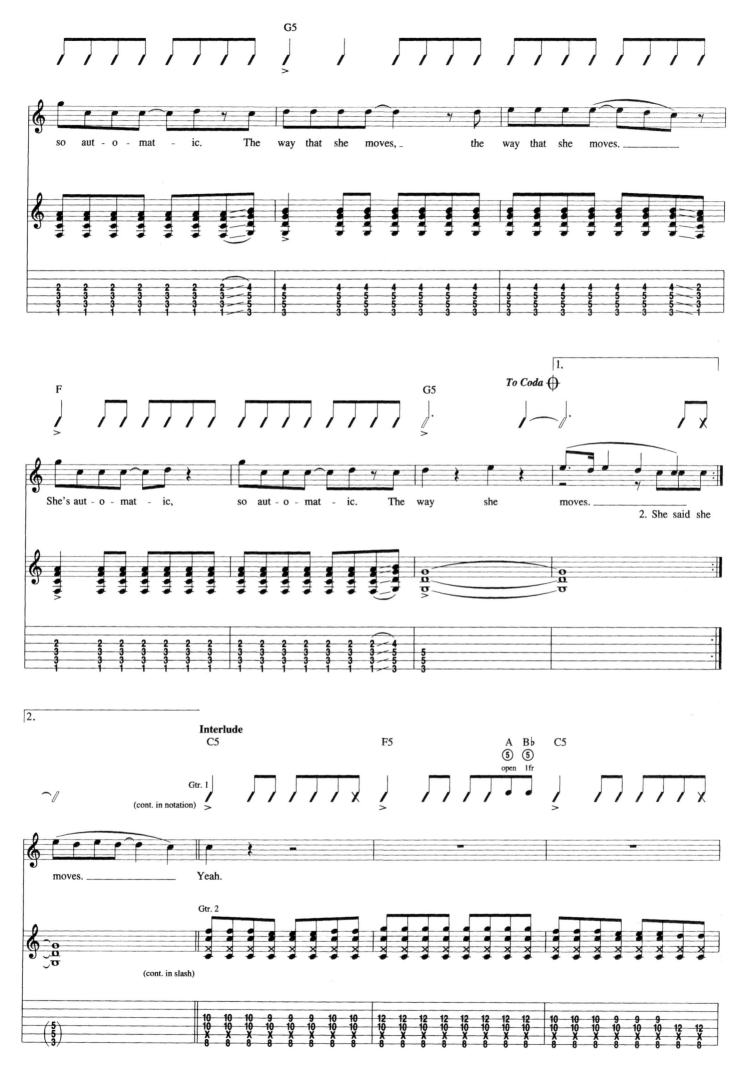

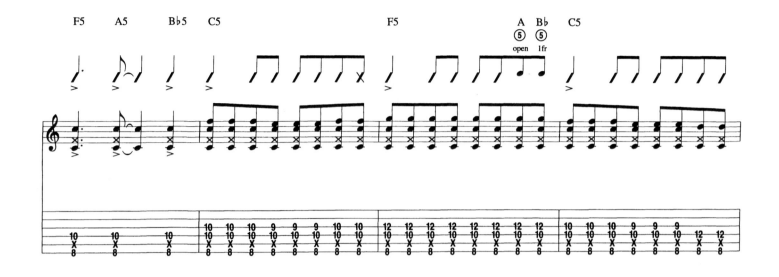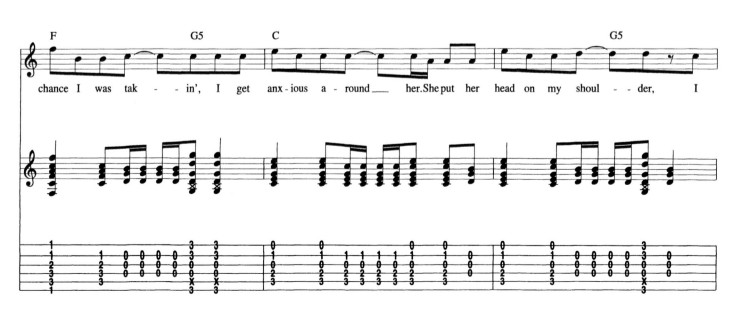

Old Friend

Words and Music by Tim Armstrong, Matt Freeman and Lars Frederiksen

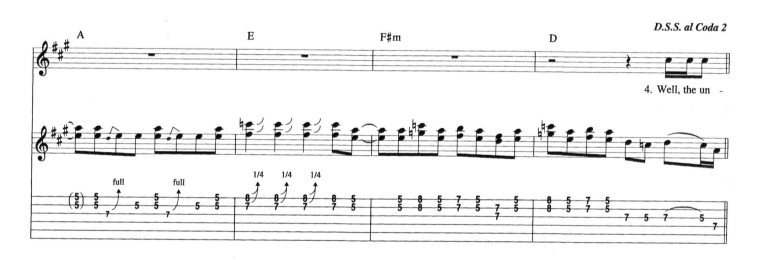
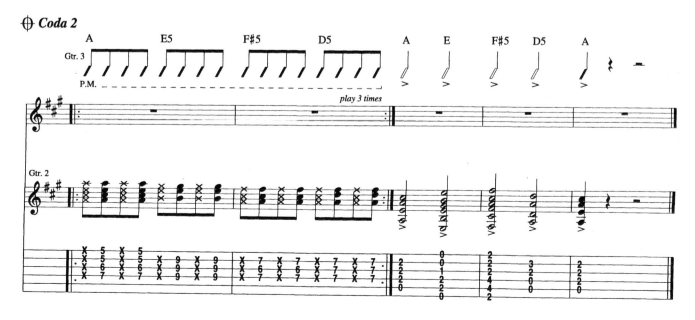

Disorder and Disarray

Words and Music by Tim Armstrong, Matt Freeman and Lars Frederiksen

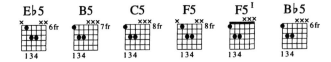

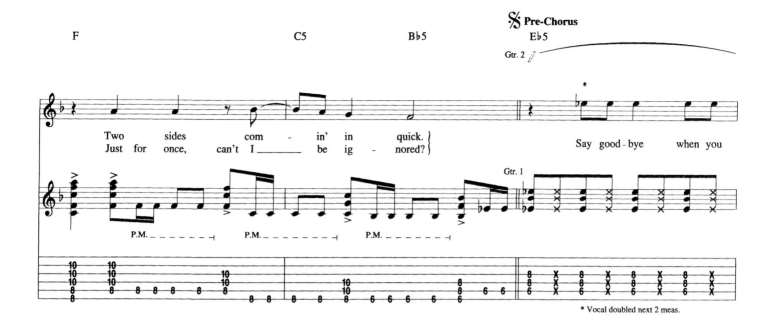

* Vocal doubled next 2 meas.

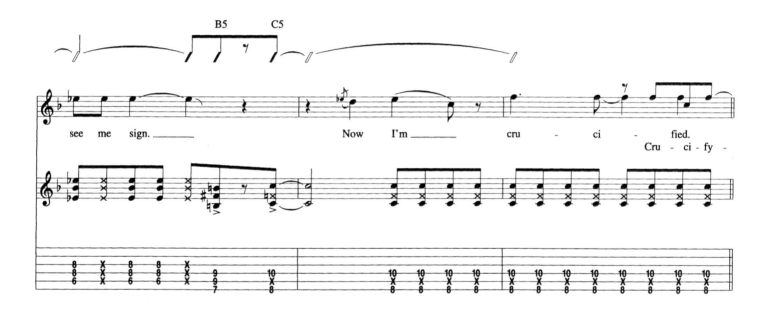

Chorus
Gtrs. 1 & 2: w/ Rhy. Fig. 1, 4 times

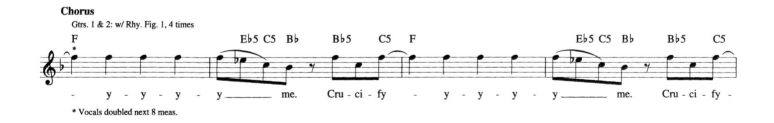

* Vocals doubled next 8 meas.

3rd time, To Coda 1
4th time, To Coda 2

65

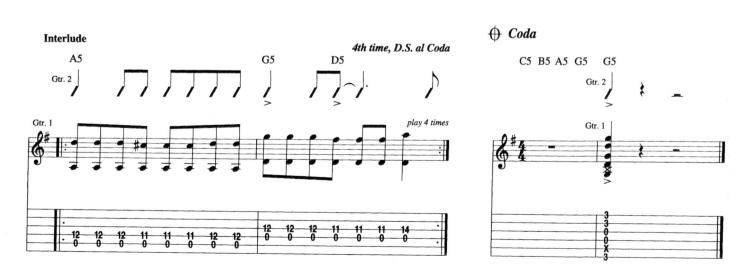

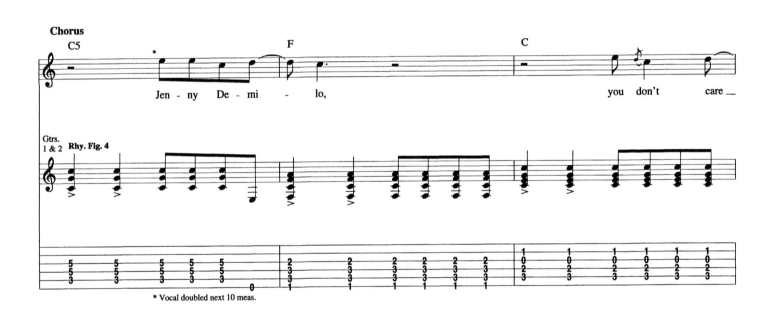

Avenues & Alleyways

Words and Music by Tim Armstrong, Matt Freeman and Lars Frederiksen

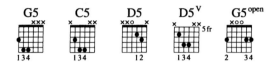

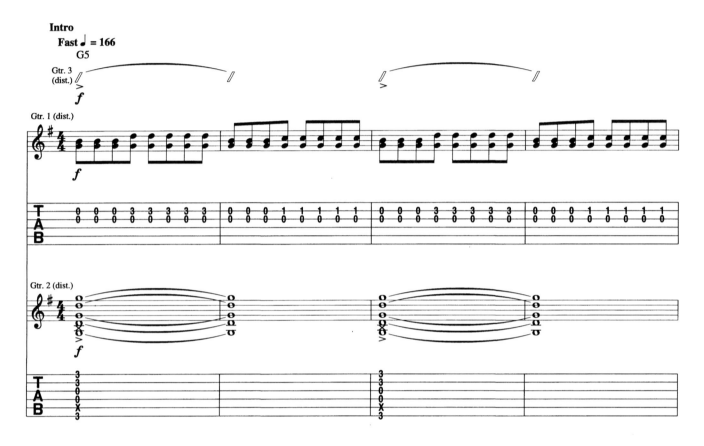

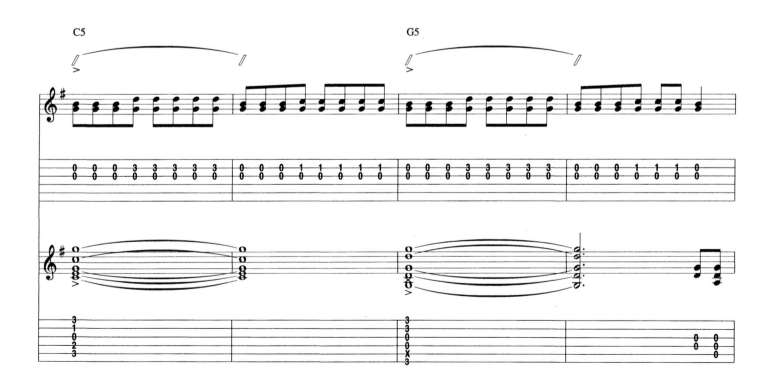

Copyright © 1995 I Want To Go Where The Action Is Music (BMI)
All Rights Administered by Wixen Music Publishing, Inc.
International Copyright Secured   All Rights Reserved

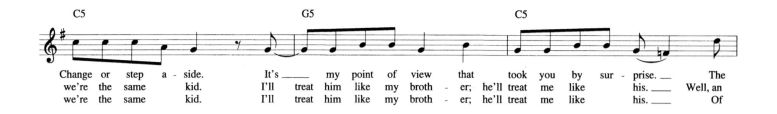
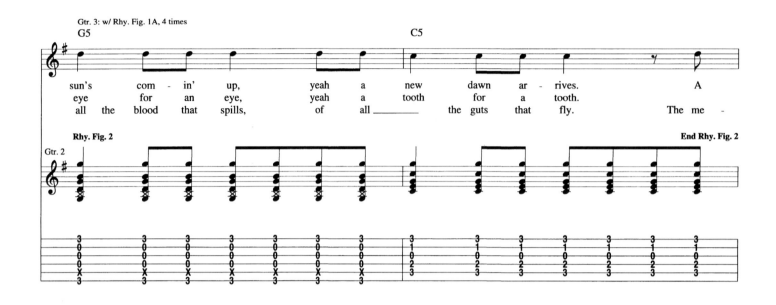
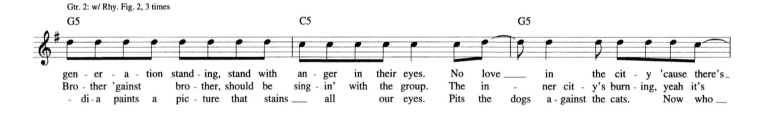
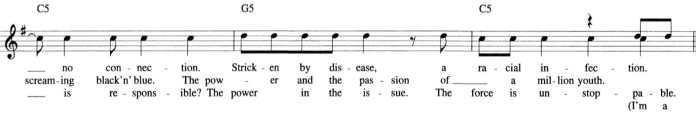
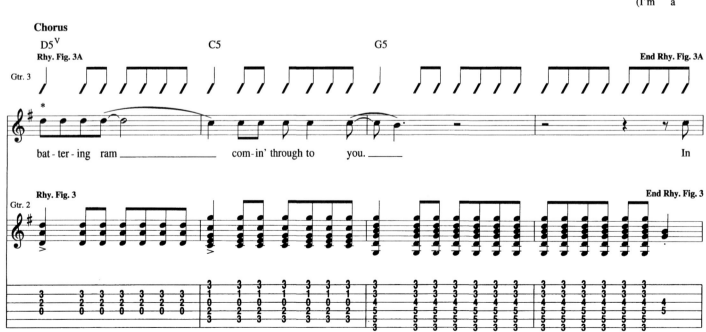

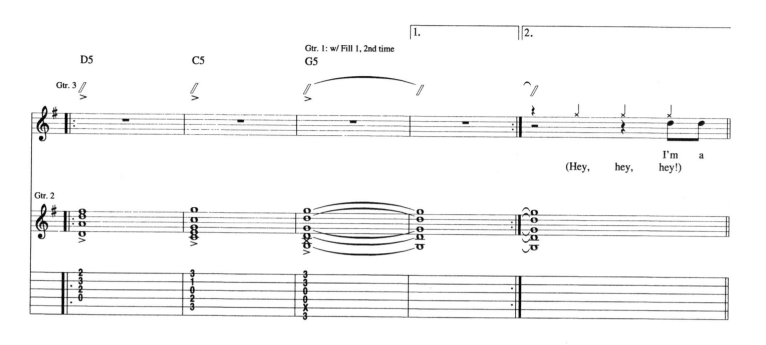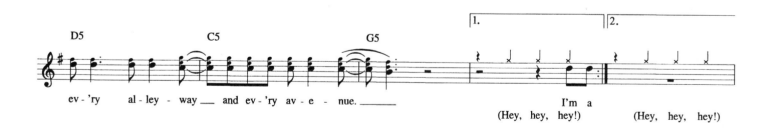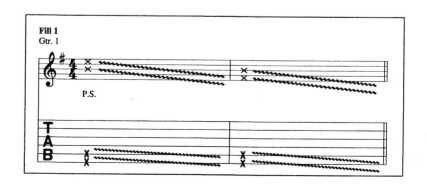

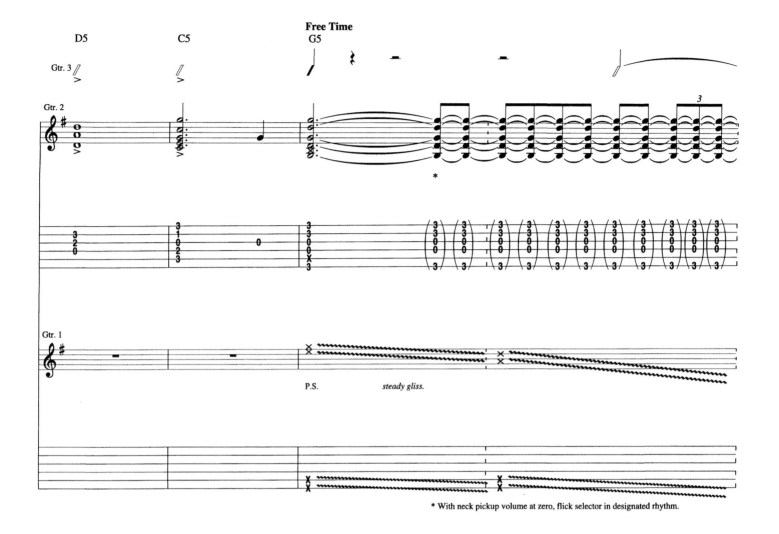
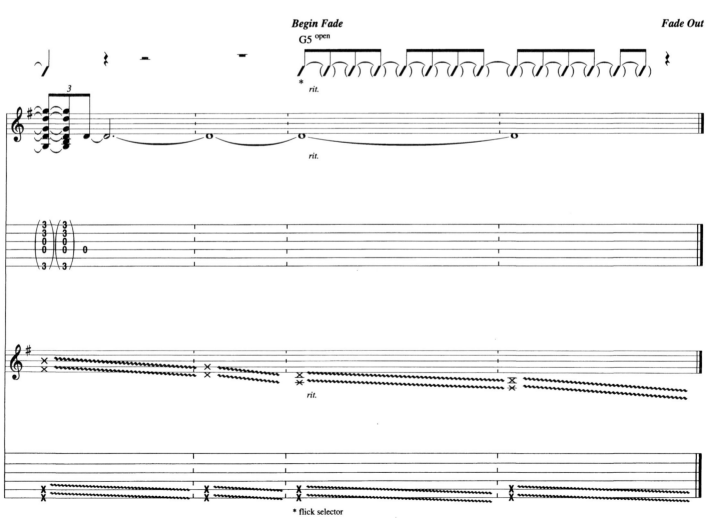

The Way I Feel
Words and Music by Tim Armstrong, Matt Freeman and Lars Frederiksen

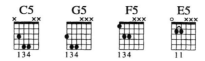

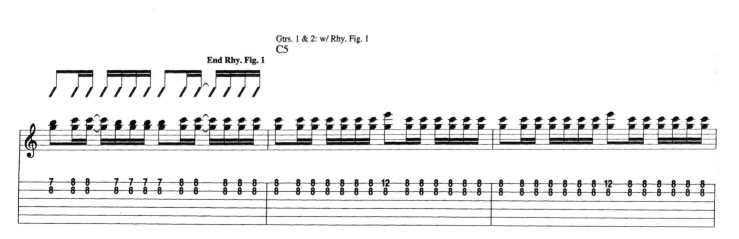

Copyright © 1995 I Want To Go Where The Action Is Music (BMI)
All Rights Administered by Wixen Music Publishing, Inc.
International Copyright Secured   All Rights Reserved

Adina

Words and Music by Tim Armstrong and Matt Freeman

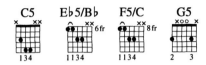

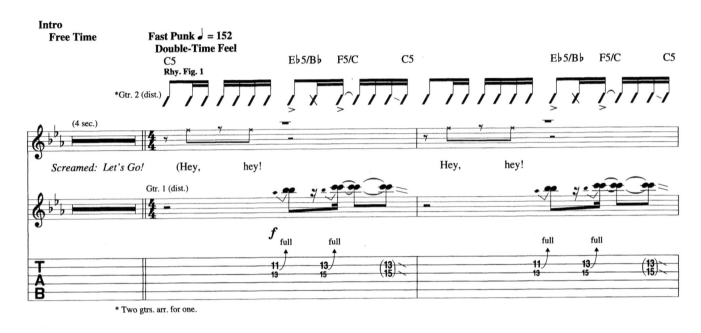

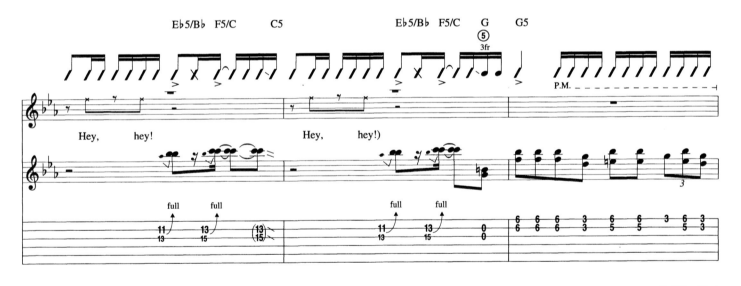

Copyright © 1993 Rancid Music
International Copyright Secured   All Rights Reserved

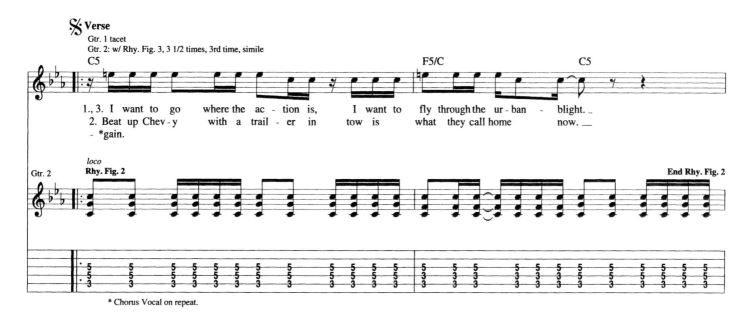

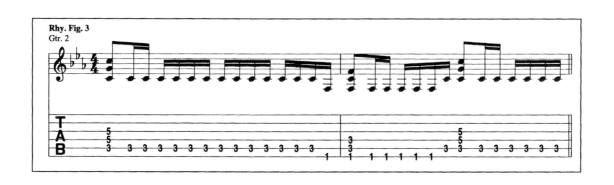

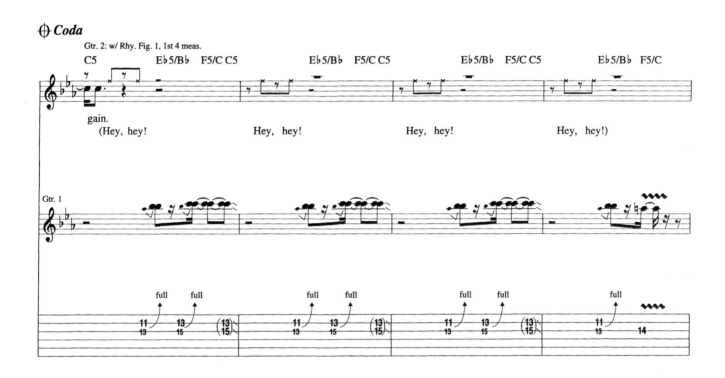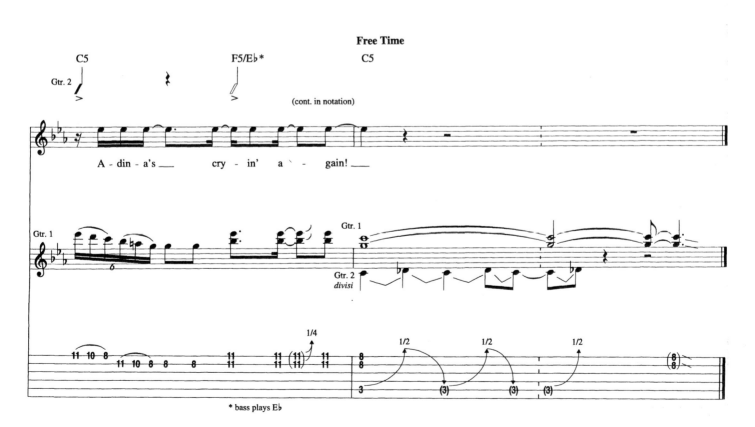

Nihilism

Words and Music by Tim Armstrong, Matt Freeman and Lars Frederiksen

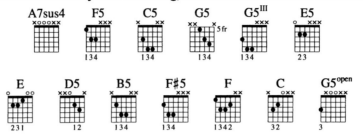

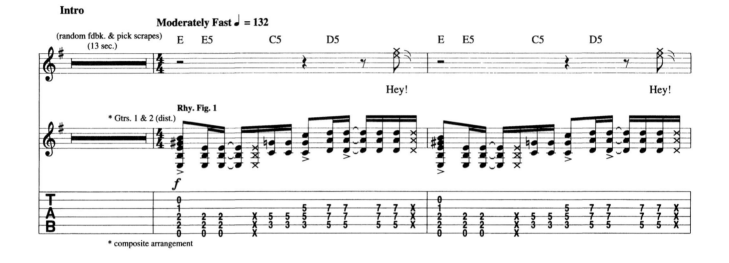

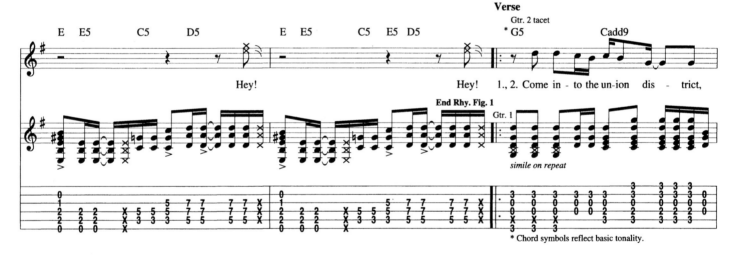

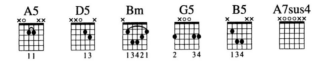

Side Kick

Words and Music by Tim Armstrong and Matt Freeman

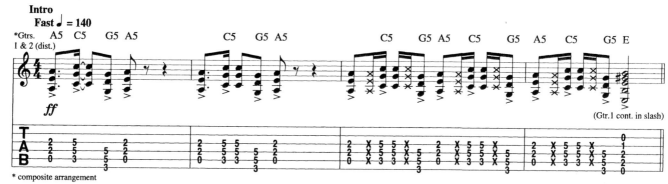

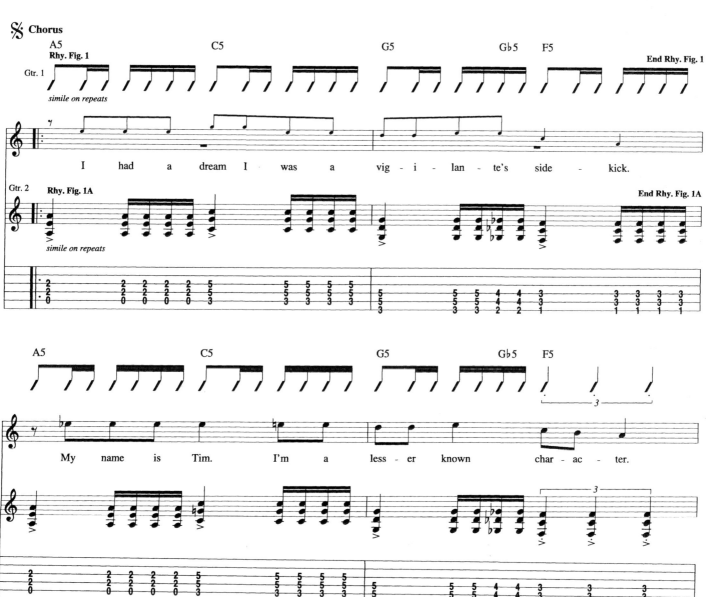

Salvation

Words and Music by Tim Armstrong and Matt Freeman

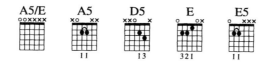

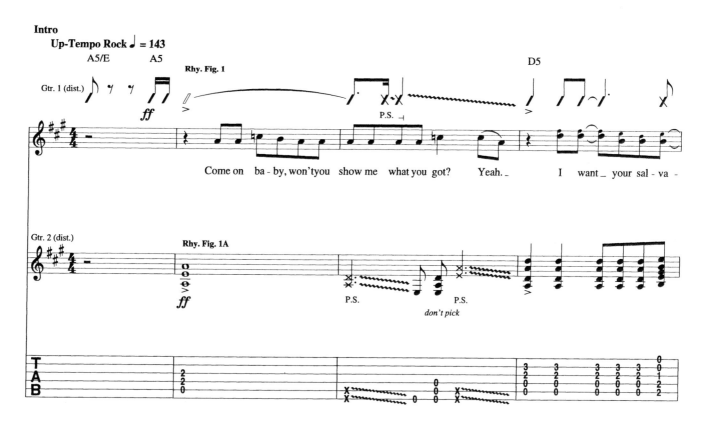

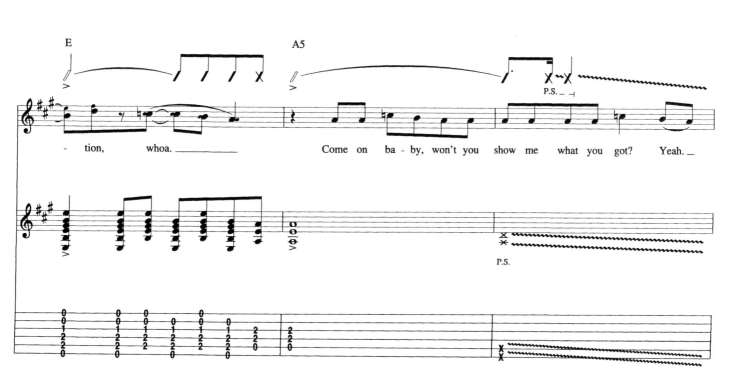

Copyright © 1994 Rancid Music
International Copyright Secured   All Rights Reserved

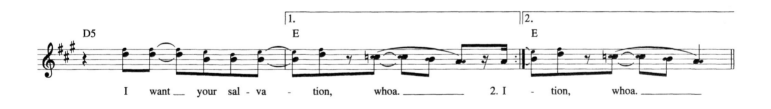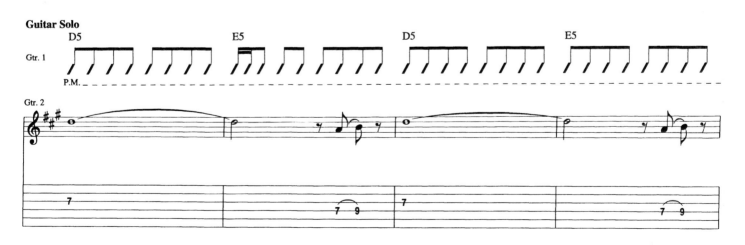

The Ballad of Jimmy & Johnny

Words and Music by Tim Armstrong and Matt Freeman

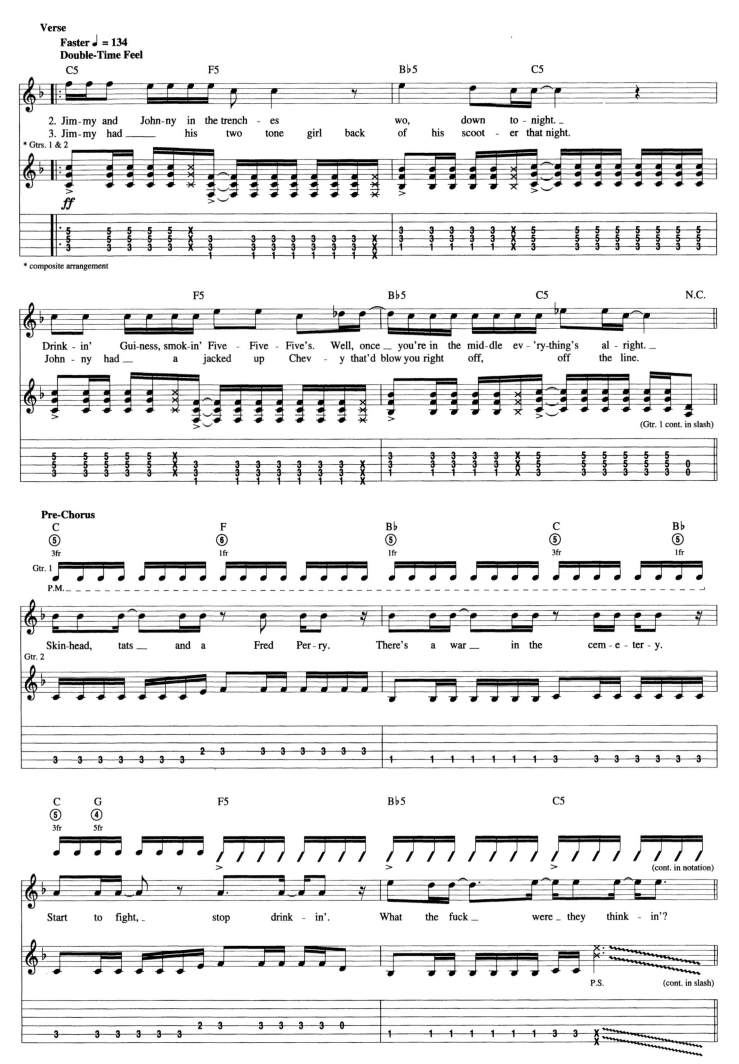

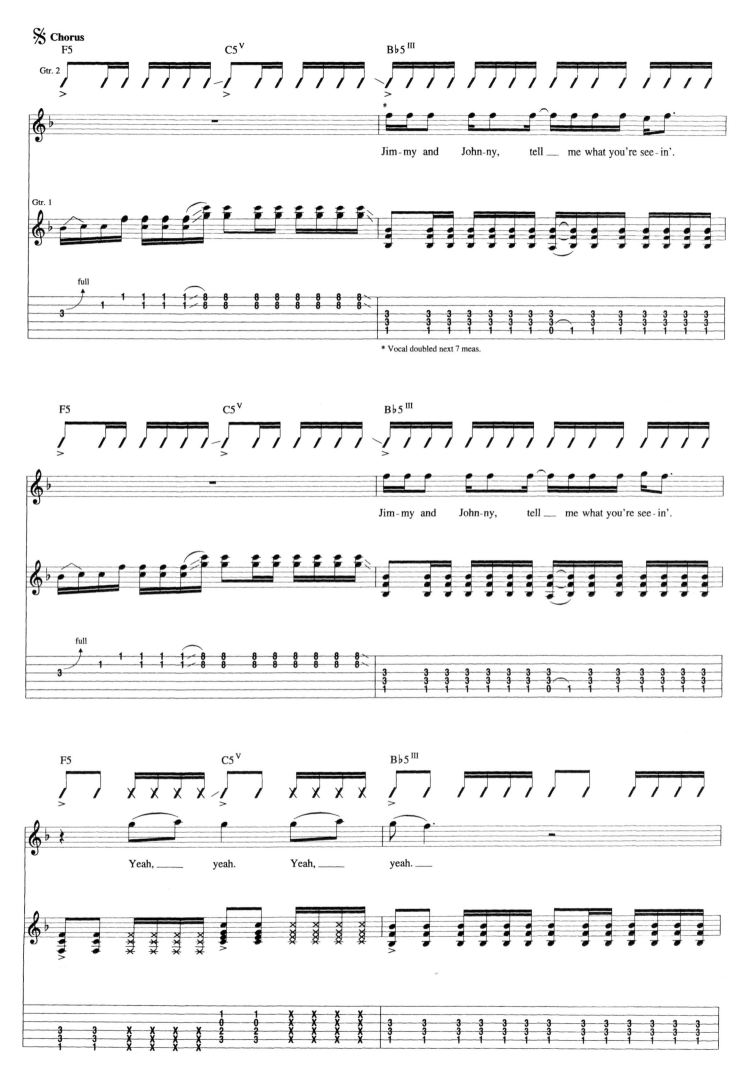

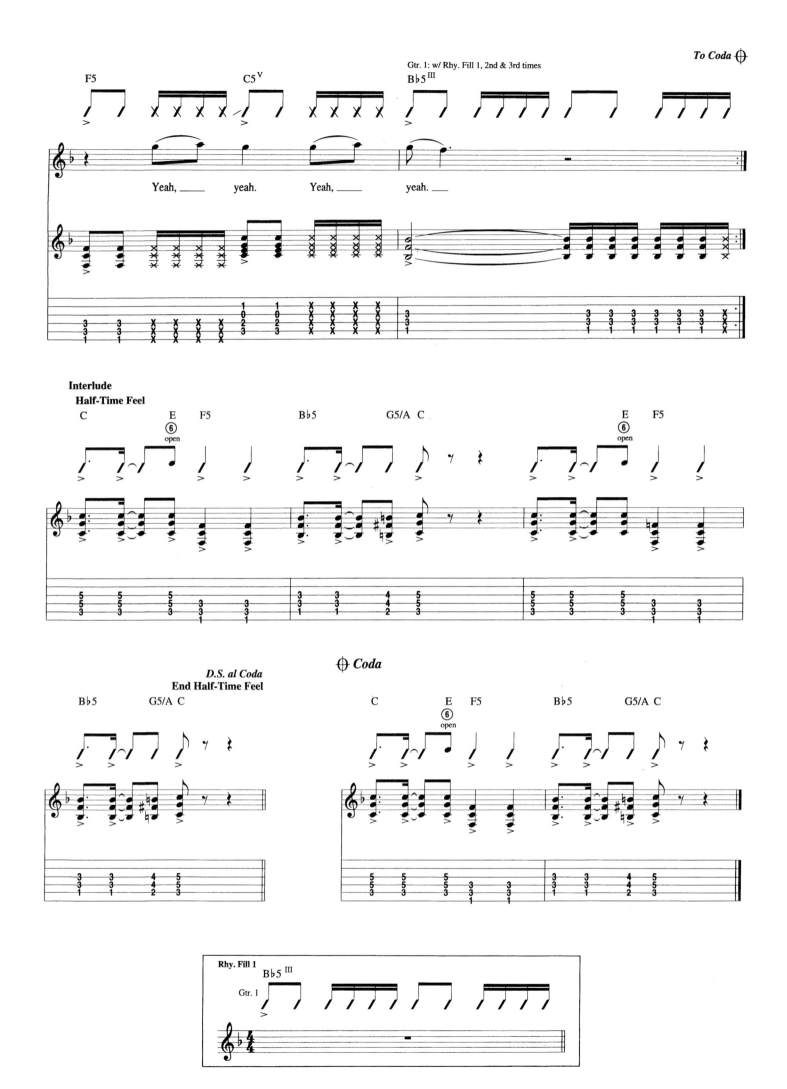

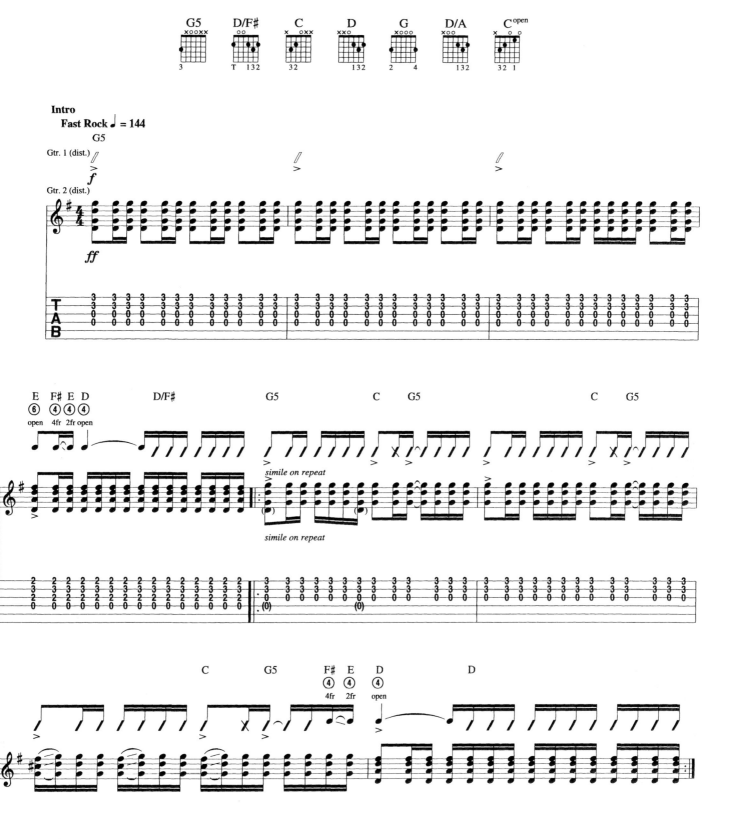

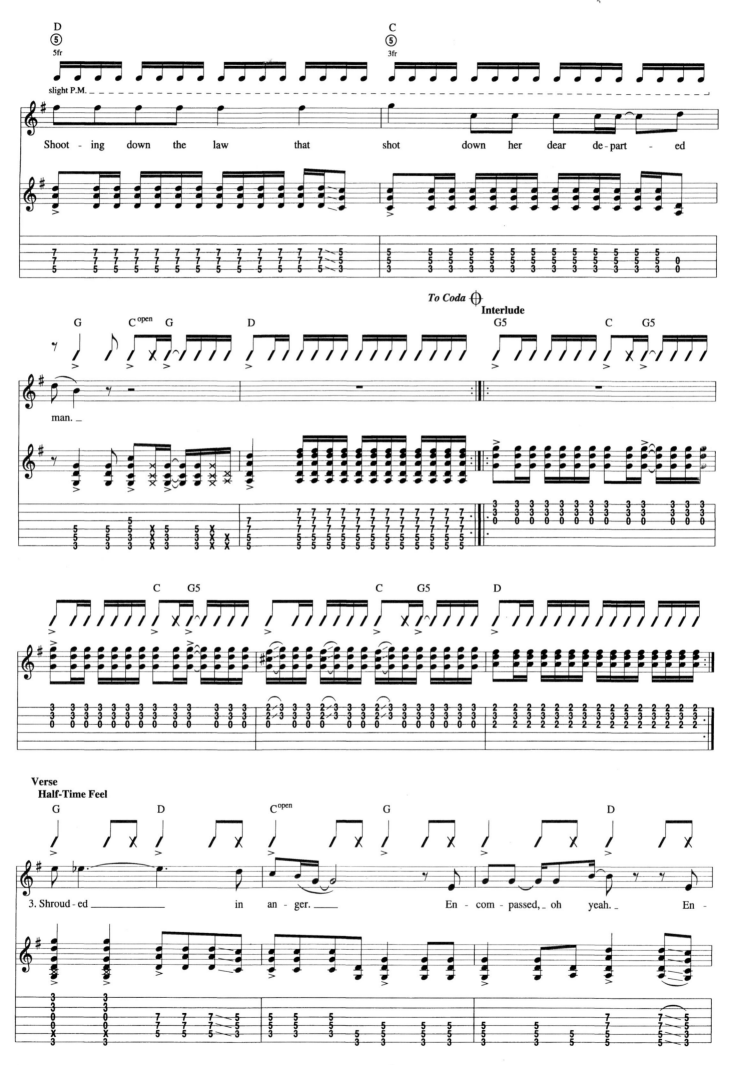

Guitar Notation Legend

Guitar Music can be notated three different ways: on a *musical staff*, in *tablature*, and in *rhythm slashes*.

RHYTHM SLASHES are written above the staff. Strum chords in the rhythm indicated. Use the chord diagrams found at the top of the first page of the transcription for the appropriate chord voicings. Round noteheads indicate single notes.

THE MUSICAL STAFF shows pitches and rhythms and is divided by bar lines into measures. Pitches are named after the first seven letters of the alphabet.

TABLATURE graphically represents the guitar fingerboard. Each horizontal line represents a string, and each number represents a fret.

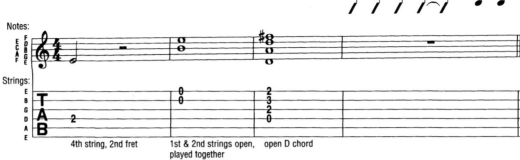

HALF-STEP BEND: Strike the note and bend up 1/2 step.

WHOLE-STEP BEND: Strike the note and bend up one step.

GRACE NOTE BEND: Strike the note and bend up as indicated. The first note does not take up any time.

SLIGHT (MICROTONE) BEND: Strike the note and bend up 1/4 step.

BEND AND RELEASE: Strike the note and bend up as indicated, then release back to the original note. Only the first note is struck.

PRE-BEND: Bend the note as indicated, then strike it.

VIBRATO: The string is vibrated by rapidly bending and releasing the note with the fretting hand.

WIDE VIBRATO: The pitch is varied to a greater degree by vibrating with the fretting hand.

HAMMER-ON: Strike the first (lower) note with one finger, then sound the higher note (on the same string) with another finger by fretting it without picking.

PULL-OFF: Place both fingers on the notes to be sounded. Strike the first note and without picking, pull the finger off to sound the second (lower) note.

LEGATO SLIDE: Strike the first note and then slide the same fret-hand finger up or down to the second note. The second note is not struck.

SHIFT SLIDE: Same as legato slide, except the second note is struck.

TRILL: Very rapidly alternate between the notes indicated by continuously hammering on and pulling off.

TAPPING: Hammer ("tap") the fret indicated with the pick-hand index or middle finger and pull off to the note fretted by the fret hand.

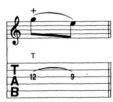

NATURAL HARMONIC: Strike the note while the fret-hand lightly touches the string directly over the fret indicated.

PINCH HARMONIC: The note is fretted normally and a harmonic is produced by adding the edge of the thumb or the tip of the index finger of the pick hand to the normal pick attack.

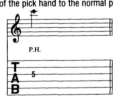

PICK SCRAPE: The edge of the pick is rubbed down (or up) the string, producing a scratchy sound.

MUFFLED STRINGS: A percussive sound is produced by laying the fret hand across the string(s) without depressing, and striking them with the pick hand.

PALM MUTING: The note is partially muted by the pick hand lightly touching the string(s) just before the bridge.

RAKE: Drag the pick across the strings indicated with a single motion.

TREMOLO PICKING: The note is picked as rapidly and continuously as possible.

VIBRATO BAR DIVE AND RETURN: The pitch of the note or chord is dropped a specified number of steps (in rhythm) then returned to the original pitch.

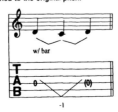

VIBRATO BAR SCOOP: Depress the bar just before striking the note, then quickly release the bar.

VIBRATO BAR DIP: Strike the note and then immediately drop a specified number of steps, then release back to the original pitch.